MW00760813

A Poet's Decree

To Marty,
Pochetta

From Paul H. Brown

Love, ...
Blessings!

12-22-16

A Poet's Decree

Rhythm of Life

Pamela M. Young

Kingdom Living Publishing
Accokeek, Maryland

Copyright © 2016 Pamela M. Young

All rights reserved under International Copyright Law. No part of this book may be reproduced or transmitted in any form or by any means, except for the inclusion of brief quotations in reviews, without permission in writing from the Publisher.

Article on page 55 reprinted courtesy of *The Goldsboro News Argus*. Reprinted with permission.

Cover design by TLH Designs, Chicago, IL
www.tlhdesigns.com

Published by Kingdom Living Publishing
P.O. Box 660
Accokeek, MD 20607
www.kingdomlivingbooks.com

Printed in the United States of America.
ISBN 978-0 -9968089-1-0

Dedication

I thank my Lord and Savior Jesus Christ for inspiring *A Poet's Decree*. It has been an inevitable journey that I could not have seen with my eyes alone; nor can I tell the route in which I've arrived. I thank God I'm here and assume not to chase the wind. Blessings are in abundance in every line, on every page; they fill me as though I've eaten my favorite food; but the bread of life. I honor my father in heaven with the highest praise, alleluia for revealing and sharing with me in quiet time, in dreams, and life. I am certain of *A Poet's Decree* because it was written by my Father and me. Thank you Jesus!

Acknowledgments

To my mother Mrs. Edna M. Young, I dedicate *A Poet's Decree*. This poem is dedicated to you, my mother.

Extraordinary Mother

My mother is a gift, God's manifestation
A woman that bore life that was already given
She nurtured four boys to men
And raised two women
Seems the simplest of times when we were children
As we are older seems much clearer
You couldn't buy the pace that kept her near us
An extraordinary woman
Who settled in her spirit and it was done
She would have respect from her children
As her words were born
And respect did trickle and cadence everyone
Sound was the foundation the legacy of our lives
To see my oldest brother obey
Was to each of us twice
She stays the course even unto this day

The cadence of life do honor her this way
For we express what is, what has been done
By an extraordinary woman
Ms. Edna M. Young

I give thanks to the offspring of my mother: Michael Lane, MSgt. Charles H. Lane Jr., Felecia A. Tucker, Elgin J. Lane, and Elder Darren Young for support and many cherished moments by God we shared exemplified in life **our rhythm to bear.**

A *Poet's Decree* is written in memory of my father, the late William Alexander Mitchell Sr.

From My Heartbeat

When I remember my father
I don't have to go far
The gist of his spirit is right near my heart
His smile and presence rings many bells
Even brings the day he said it this way
The place and attire that makes it all the same
The memories of my father
Oh what a time, all that I can conjure
And know they're all mine
I'm thankful for this day that I can travel such places
To know and remember his expressions and faces
Yes
In memory of you I write

"A Poet's Decree"
Certainly I remember
What you mean to me
As I will the next time
I breathe a breath of poetry

I give thanks to the offspring of my father: Reverend Dr. William Alexander Mitchell Jr., Malcolm Keith Mitchell, Timothy E. Mitchell, Sandra G. Bizzell, Lenora Mitchell, Juanita Whitfield, Barbara Rogers, and Judy F. Mojica for the rhythm we bear and continual days rather near or far and how we always give God the praise!

The unity of family is exemplified throughout the Bible and is honorable to be respected as such. Family is where I exercise the schematics of life, where my morals and values begin. I believe every problem can be solved if you go back to the beginning, making its meaning very significant. Therefore, the beginning of respect is at home, the beginning of loyalty is at home; the beginning of comfort is at home; the beginning of support is at home. I am completed by my family.

To Reverend Dr. William J. Barber II, a man of great demeanor, whom I respect dearly, thank you for writing the foreword for *"A Poet's Decree"* and your support from the very beginning. I'm thankful for the God in you that gives me confirmation of His kindred spirit. These are the realms that God has blessed us to travel in His name to be identified as such and I am certain of your part in this journey; that it is ordained by God. Thank you!

Table of Contents

Foreword

The prophets of the Bible were poets. The hymn writers of the church are poets. Poetry is that unique gift of being able to find the rhyme, rhythm, and melody of life itself. Poets turn our ears into eyes. Poets express the movement of living through the words they pen. In our joys, the poets are there. In the pain of life, the poets are there. Listen to the lyrics lifted by the voice of Mahalia Jackson or the preaching of Martin Luther King and you hear in them the spirit of the poets. Within these pages are the words of another poet who dares to listen to the rhythm of life and write what she hears and feels, and once again as so many have before her... turn our ears into eyes.

Reverend Dr. William J. Barber II, Pastor
Greenleaf Christian Church
Goldsboro, North Carolina

Breath of a Poet

The Ultimate Reaping

Oftentimes we associate reaping as a synonym for being punished for wrong doings (we reap what we sow). However, it's extremely more vast than we can imagine. I've been blessed to have humbly realized myself and made available to reap my very own being. Are you aware that we reap ourselves in affiliation with others? If you can't deal with yourself, then why would you want someone else to have to deal with you? Take the test, spend time with yourself, and see how long it takes for you to get on your own nerves. Be honest with yourself, and then think of those in affiliation with you (companions, friends, family). Now, how much more consideration will you have in regards to others having to deal with your unnerving characteristics, the way we behave around others, your presence, yourself? The ultimate reaping conjures forgiveness, 20/20 vision of reflection, wrongs that can be made right, acceptance and forgiveness of oneself. Then, we are put in a position of healing and are made stronger. Moving on with your life is in abundant light! We also reap events in our lives that we repress and camouflage with people, places, and things. When we remove camouflages, rather it's a person, place, or thing; the good, the bad, and the ugly; if left along long enough, you will see yourself with no choice but to deal with yourself or continue to repeat yourself. We all have sides to us that we oftentimes assume not to acknowledge. Rather we assume to be passive, concluding that we're not so bad after all. Or, I really don't need to change this side of me. I can get away with being like this, if I just overlook myself. Deep down inside we know our shortcomings and inadequacies that stipulate our growth in life. Overlooking yourself is like saying, you don't exist (you truly can't lie to yourself). I chose to look in the mirror, forced to heal from hiding in repression and camouflages I had allowed to covet emotions I didn't want to deal with or acknowledge. Now I'm available for myself and more aware of the affects I have on other people because of the characteristics I possess, acknowledging myself, and being empowered by chance and change by the grace of God. There're so many people looking for themselves and don't even know they don't know themselves. They go their whole life never being introduced to whom they are, because they are afraid of being alone. Ask me how I know… I was afraid of being alone, too. People are camouflaged by the spirit of their peers. When we enter this world we are surrounded by people. Our nature is not to be alone. How do we break away from nature to find who we are? By grace, I'm finding who I am ultimately, not by sole choice, but my desire for His will in my life. Grace found me wanting to be more, seeing myself, and looking in the mirror.

Introduction

Compassion

My eyes filled with tears
As my heart broke
She spoke words piercing my ears
I couldn't believe the inhumanity
Of humanity
I called out to Jesus, yielding no choice
Hear my cry, hear my voice
I can't believe the depths a man will go
Just to have more
No matter how much bad he sows
To achieve a thing in monetary gain
And in the end, have not a friend
I send a word to permeate the atmosphere
To those that read and those that hear
Know that Jesus is Lord
It is wise to fear
Not a man standing in himself
Praying upon the unfortunate
To obtain a greater wealth
A woman at the time
Who could do no better
Forced to compromise
A situation she despised
Having to make ends meet
She chose to turn the other cheek

Certainly it isn't over, it can't be done
There's nothing new under the sun
We reap what we sow, sow a good seed
Whatever it is, it will come back indeed

Conning Emotions

Certainly, we correlate to heart-to-heart conversation. When we understand one another, we feel each other's sentiments. It soothes the psyche and encourages a release in satisfied emotions that comfort your person. On the other hand, we also can correlate to a motivator whom encouraging words stimulate another's desires. One who is acting upon words with emotions that have no true feeling behind it, but a premeditated approach to achieve or obtain certain personal gain. You are a pun in fulfillment, while your emotions are being conned through and by entertaining your desires (being manipulated). Ask me how I know… It happened to me and I dared to learn from being someone's pun to control, satisfying their personal gain, while the repetition of their words became as an overseer of slaves (taunting). It's amazing to understand, some of the time, the person delivering the message, doesn't apply the same approach to themselves or neither practice what they've preached. We all for the most part, can talk the truth and it's the unadulterated truth. However, I've experienced a motivator who manipulated and moved another in a seemingly positive direction because of their words, but did not apply the same approach to their own life to the point that they made progress themselves. They just said what needed to be heard to obtain a greater gain (manipulating). Preying upon the seemingly weak was the approach. As I sort through my words today; I've identified and am sharing with the world the evils of a man or woman with no good intent. What was meant for my bad has been set aside for my good. I'm telling a story that I overcame that which tried to overcome me. My prayer is that it helps another you see. If I had to close, I guess I would say conning emotions had its way; God forbid I would continue to be prey. So, let my words bless now and be a recollection to you later.

Wolves in Sheep's Clothing

Many shall come in my name saying, I am Christ
And shall deceive many, even the very elect
If it were possible
Prophesying of His goodness, claiming His name
Appearing to be holy
A practice that has been perfected, enticing the senses
With aromatic smells
Having a form of godliness, but denying the power thereof
The sight with a deception of divinity,
Preying upon the desiring heart
And the weakness of the flesh, initiating contact
Through vulnerability
A preying eye that has sought you out
Beware, these are the beginning of sorrows and reasons
And deliverance
For many are called, but few are chosen
And unto the chosen was a seed planted deep within
A spiritual accolade known since before time
And earths to come
A heavenly stamp that says, touch not my anointed
Allowed me to walk through the storm with this reason
To write unto the saints
I turned and told the devil, I am free
Because Jesus paid it all for me
As was in my dream I am sustained by faith
And my belief in God

For it is written, every deity or being
Has to walk around me
Because they can't touch me
I have been delivered unto this page and into your life
To make you aware of a trap that has been called out
And weakened as of this day through knowledge
That is most powerful
And love that I hope exudes off the pages
Into a blessing in your life
Then I would have by the grace of God made a difference
Making my significance just
Amen

Political Poetry

America

I guess this America where the rich give Rolls Royces
As gifts
And the poor wonder where their next meal
Is coming from

I guess this is America where over three hundred million
Dollar airbus planes are built to seat four hundred
And minorities cannot afford a ticket

I guess this is America where our soldiers
Were sent out to fight a war
Declared by a president who cannot answer
A direct question

I guess this is America where they take
The nutrients out of food
And sell it right back to us in high end whole food stores

I guess this is America where you live in the projects on
welfare
When you get a job they raise your rent leaving no room
for improvement

I guess this is America where one percent of Americans
Strive and thrive
While ninety-nine percent pay for the ride

I guess this is America where In God We Trust
Is written on our currency
And there are those who kill, steal, and destroy to get it

I guess this is America
Is this America
Land of the free, home of the brave

I guess this is America

The Second Man

The Saga Continues

He's bigger than I thought, understood, and knew
By the grace of God, I'm destined to get through
A premeditated trap by another man's hand
Concentrated diligently so another can't stand
On his own two feet and say I'm a man
Or an independent woman
By another man's hand
As I live and breathe, I've begun to see
How this plot thickens for you and me
Knowledge is power, so let's get some
It's not meant for us to achieve
But to break our spirit, so we don't believe
The Willie Lynch theory is still alive
In another form giving wind to thrive
If not recognized be strengthened too
By the ignorance of a race
Who thinks it's through
Weaken their minds, keep their bodies strong
In the 21st century it's still going on
A bondage that has been manifested physically
Breaking the spirits of many
Sifting into families, generation to generation
Swim my child through the thickness
Overlapping circumstances

Mitigating factors
Pending investigations
Do you qualify
Does a felon live in your home
If so check this box
Not even a chance, already at the bottom
Am I my brother's keeper
I guess I am
Who are you, rude and aggressive
The second man
I await his exit

Politics with Fairer Market Fame

It shall come to pass
We will have a government for the people
Elected by the people
Politics with fairer market fame
As was in my dream those very words
It shall come to pass that a black man
Will become president
He will govern the nation for the people
Unbiased in his approach, favoring all mankind
There will be things to come to pass
That has never before been seen
We are living in historic times where the universe
Is coming full circle
Time is about to change as we know it
Chains are being broken
Prophesies are being fulfilled
The last shall be first, and the first shall be last
We are in the midst of a racial reaping
That cannot be stopped
The will that drives this change is stronger than man
Even stronger than life
For so long man thought he controlled change
For so long it seemed like he did
But there is a way that seems right unto man
The end thereof is destruction

This time is greater than any man
Our destinies are ultimately out of our hands
We are mere mortals of the Master's plan
Can't man nor woman, change, interfere, or disrupt what
God has sanctioned
We will begin to see with our own eyes
Who is for us and who is not
The hidden vessels that oppress change
That would benefit us all
Those who lobby for a select few are about to feel
The sting of the just
For they knew all along this time would come
An unveiling of the unrighteous, deceitful
Manipulative minds of the government
For we shall survive politics with fairer market fame
In this day

Voters

We dream of a day we correlate
Appreciating a government we help make
By casting our votes, every man, woman,
Black, green, or white
Making a change in spite…of our color, creed, or gender
Making a difference when our votes we tender
However, the outcome, we made a move
To make a difference and encourage change
If we don't vote, it will stay the same
However, the candidate that achieves the office
We made a stand and should be proud
That we didn't sit back and be part of the crowd
That didn't vote and have a lot to say
When their opinion doesn't matter this way
We all have a voice and should be heard
So cast your vote and spread the word
Your opinion matters
When the votes they gather
And you've had your say on election day

Election Night 2008

I feel an anointed spirit of change
My spirit is weakened by intense humility
That stretches from the beginning of my ancestors
To my very existence
Deeper than my senses can feel
Farther than I've ever been
Long ago before my time
Immense revelations of truth
Quiet and soothing as it drizzles rain
A calm mist and a feeling of change
Martin Luther had a dream
Prophesying of day when a man will be judged
By the content of his character
Rather than the color of his skin
Many have prayed and wept for change to come
It has come full circle, answering the prayers of many
Who have gone on to glory, paving the way for all to see
Barack Obama made history
In two thousand and eight
Became president of the United States

A Poet's Decree

Philosophical Poetry

Harvest Time

It's not that we don't have faith or we don't believe; we have to understand *why* then we can receive. When we understand the purpose of our harvest to come and tap into the treasures that is within us, our destiny will begin to release. For every release there is revelation that elevates our spiritual growth, a touch that gives birth to a newness in us which will change our lives instantaneously. To be in a place to hear God makes us in an instant a vessel to be used of God. If this were not so, there would be no revelation. We are mysteries to be understood. Only by our Father can we see ourselves. This is why we must seek Him and all these things will be added unto us. God wants to show us the purpose of what we desire, to be used ultimately to lift His kingdom. There's a spiritual reason for our carnal blessings. Knowing why disciplines us to respect the blessings of God, allowing us to be able to handle the harvest. When we learn and receive understanding, then the doors of heaven are opened. Your blessings will be unknown to man for they will not be able to fathom your inheritance, being your circumstance doesn't fit the means to your success in life. You will begin to walk in the supernatural, blessed of God having unlocked the doors to your blessings with the key of understanding *why*.

Poetic Prophecies

Our desires aren't just the things we verbally ask God for
They're the things we think in our hearts
The desires of our hearts are manifested in two parts
Innately, the desires of our heart and the spoken word

I smelled a woman's perfume as she passed by. The essence
was delightful and rich (distinguished) I thought, I desired
some perhaps.

See and understand why and whatever it is will be added
to you

My key is to know my desires are not just verbal, they're
my heart's as well, opening the door of understanding;
God blesses in two parts. Learning and understanding
without opening my mouth; I will have that perfume
because it is my desire. We must know *why*.

Why is the key! *Why* is to know there're blessings
unstressed/unspoken of. God blesses us in understanding
our spiritual purpose for a plutonic thing.

- Until understanding is found, blessings aren't
released, because of unpreparedness
to handle the blessing. I'm a Christian, I believe; why
haven't I received?

A Poet's Decree

- You have to first become available for God and
  He will teach and reveal your *why*. Then your
  inheritance will come, your **spiritual reason** for your
  plutonic thing.

Rise Above Your Classification

I was put in a box before I was born
A spiritual war I would have to fight even
Before I learned to walk
Demonic spirits of oppression lurking from sweet songs
Of slave owners
And their descendants who have carried
The torch of racism
Perpetuating supremacy and inadequacies
From birth to seniority
A legacy of hatred that has beguiled their offspring
Aborting chance, change, and opportunity
For a righteous seed to spring forth
A spiritual stronghold by the same cause
Labeled and stipulated a race that was torn
Into mental abandonment
Rapped by mere words
That would suggest failure on sight
This is the way they did it back then
My father was a Negro and so was my mother
The rest was white, American Indian, or other
As I looked at my birth certificate
From the State Of North Carolina
I took a trip back in time to a day when
It must have been hard to be my parents
Even harder to be black, as an African American woman
In 2008

I felt the lingering stretch of oppressive rape
And anger that stemmed from the sting of a name
That labeled my parents and me all the same
It was done to them and unto me, I carry a torch
That burns unto my face
When I'm able to see, the torch burns for me
Not an accolade by any means, just a burden it seems
Of racial injustice
Until someone touches this; it will continue to be injustice
This reminds me of inequality, not just for me
But for all who came before me
This all came to be
Because of what was required of me
My birth certificate

Delivered

Some time passed and I experienced some emotions from
the past that came without a familiar trigger. I wondered
where it came from. I understand that God sustains and
keeps us if you're honest and sincere about being kept,
He will keep you. Being delivered has reference that will
sustain you in future instances opposed to the concept of
quitting which references a poem I wrote "Quitting Again."
Quitting has no strong reason, just an idea and a will that
can be weakened and quitting resumes not to exist. On the
other hand being delivered has reference, something to
refer back to that gives an account of how you overcame.
In correlation, in a different situation, I've not been able to
give an account while I know it's already done; therefore,
there're people, places, and things concerning this matter
that I choose not to associate myself with. Although this
is true I don't have the desire to associate myself because
my mind is kept on the things of God and He keeps me
exemplifying His word in my daily life. Surely, my journey
is working itself out that it may manifest a shared moment
with whoever will give ear.

A Poet's Decree

Black Is Beautiful

I've heard this phrase many times throughout my life
I encouraged myself, because the color was black,
It was beautiful
Then it was my turn; for the first time in my life
It had new meaning
With urgency the phrase became alive and masterful
A spiritual endeavor to express my heart beat
And desire that I am
Black is beautiful was defined in me
Like many who wear the brand of color
He soared from the free throw line
To six championship rings
Basketball's greatest, Michael Jordan
A native of North Carolina, a Tar Heel at best
The first of his time to achieve such a feat, a living legacy,
A part of history
Black is beautiful in my eyes I see
A Jamaican from Sherwood Content, Trelawny
Who would grow up and become
One of the most renowned track stars of our time
Shattering world records at the Diamond League games
The fastest man in the world, Usain Bolt
Black is beautiful
As I watch Venus and Serena Williams battle at Wimbledon
An esteemed honor and historical accolade

Turning in stellar performances to our athletic dismay
Two professional American sisters making history
On the tennis courts
Never before had it been seen such athletic ability
In female tennis
Black is beautiful, I thought
As I watched Barack Obama walk across the platform
As the next president of our United States
Hand in hand with his two daughters and First Lady
Michelle Obama
Wearing and ensemble of black and red
Gracing the stage in unity symbolizing our United States
Black Is Beautiful

My Man

I commend the man who mates me
He's bold and brilliant approaching me
Like his Father I'm sure
A man of his word who findeth me
His signature is upon his steps
Steps of a righteous man
Looking not as the world would
At the outward man
He sees my spirit within, and all its contingencies
Resonating the beauty in me
Many may say, "There's something about me"
But he knows me spiritually
Like his Father I'm sure, who sent him to me
Soul of my soul, flesh of my flesh
Many seek, many find
Only God can send and man divine
That mates my soul
And love is mine
He's worthy, capable, and able
We are bound by our spirit's rhythm
As Adam and Eve, right in our bellies
A part of his life, that questions no more
Delivered unto a woman that he adores
And will have as his wife, if she'd have his hand
Glory be to God
Who sent me a man

A Real Man

A real man can do what a woman can
She cooks, he cooks, she cleans, he cleans
Who ever conceived the perpetuated idea
That a man is supposed to be far from his feelings
A true man of God understands the sentiments
Of love and romance
Without interference, wisdom is delightful
When he understands her
Real men have been stolen by time
And a world that seeks to legitimize by its standards
An overlapping veil upon generations of men
Who have denied themselves in part
To a dormant and wandering heart
Whose home has been waiting patiently on its counterpart
For from his rib, she was formed, as the earth without void
A mate, exemplifying compatibility
From the Truth and the Light
Oh, how sentiments took a plight
I know a secret that lie deep within
The forbidden gates of the heart of a man
He's not much different from my heart you see
God made him, and then He made me
I know his heart, because I know mine
To every man's heart lies a love divine
Acknowledge himself and he will find

More than meets the eye, or thought could be
Standing in God's prophesy
The real man
He was put here to be

My Son

I saw my son I never had
In a dream, he was shown to me and I knew he was mine
I finally know what it feels like,
The love of a mother for her child
An emotion like an organ
In the center of my being that belongs
Gathered inside of me unified by our spirits
Explanation has no meaning, only God has the song
My baby boy, my baby boy
I saw the mountains I would move for you
As I raised and nurtured you
How your life would be different from mine
I would use all that I've learned and impart into your life
Nurture your gifts from a young age
Your intellectual wisdom from the first stage
That God has shown us from heaven above
An infant child who spoke wisdom beyond his days
When asked trivial things, it was far from his ways
The brilliance of God he displayed
My son, my son, it was nice to have met you
Even after I'm awake your spirit holds true
From the soul of your mother
I dedicate this poem to you
My son

A Poet's Decree

Inspirational Poetry

Restoration

I feel a heightened spirit within me
It is the air I smell, the breath I breathe
A new life inside of me, a life I've yet to see
It excites me, in the gist of where butterflies be
Inevitable life I see, more than me
I'm better than I could ever be
For I am in God's prophesy
He has restored me
To be all I was put here to be
Naturally
My Father and me
I see a new day coming, after a weeding out of sorts
It will seem as though the end is near for some
Because of where their treasures lie
This is a time of great faith, abundant blessings
And God's order of manifestation in the land
The righteous and upright will rise supernaturally
To higher heights in proper place
While dirt will be called dirt
Weeded out like the herbs of the field
As was in the days of Jeremiah, disobedience
By the Israelites
Caused turmoil in the land which angered God
To move in their lives
To chasten them to turn from their wicked ways
And turn their eyes back to God
After all is done, there will be calm in the land
As in the days of old
And peace again in His righteous order

Whoso endureth would've delighted himself (herself)
In the Lord
For these are trying times of restoration

Burden, GHS' first black student, dies after long battle with cancer

By Phyllis Moore

News-Argus Staff Writer

Glenwood Burden Sr., the first black student to attend Goldsboro High School on the threshold of integration in 1961, has died. He was 62.

Son Glenwood Burden Jr. said his father had been battling cancer and for the past month had been homebound. He died Thursday morning. "It really took a toll on him," Burden said. "But he was a fighter. He was in good spirits still. He passed in his sleep, didn't suffer a lot of pain."

And while his father holds a place in Goldsboro history books for being the only black student to attend the city's high school that first year, to his son he was so much more.

"He was a great, great man of character," he said. "He told us that having a great name was more important than having worldly possessions. And of course, having a relationship with God, being a man of integrity. He was a loving father, not only a father but a friend, a very close friend. He was a great example to follow."

After graduating from Goldsboro High in 1964, Burden Sr. took some classes at Wayne Community College and St. Augustine College, but left before graduating because the Vietnam War was going on and he was drafted. He joined the Navy and after four years, settled in Washington, D.C.

He returned to Wayne County in 1970, marrying the former Margaret Wilson soon after. They had two children—Burden Jr. and Valerie Bartlett of St. Louis, Mo. The couple also have six grandchildren and two great-grandchildren.

Burden held jobs as a truck driver and in retail and for a time worked at O'Berry Center. But it was through ministry that he would find his passion.

He was executive producer of Gospel Perspectives Ministries Inc., a TV program he ran for about 28 years on WHFL, Goldsboro's Christian TV station. He was also editor of the Good News Gazette, a Christian newspaper distributed throughout eastern North Carolina, for more than 14 years, and authored several booklets on "Spiritual Dimensions."

He also loved to fish and will be remembered as a "people person," his son said.

"I can recall when he had gotten sick last year, he said, 'I just want to take a ride, talk to people that I have never met before,'" he said. "He never met a stranger."

The family will meet later today to plan funeral arrangements.

Joe Faison, a long-time friend, can trace his connection with Burden Sr. back to 1972.

"We started hanging out together in a gospel group, The New Goldenaires," he said. "We had great memories together. He was a great friend of mine. We did many things together. We started the TV program together, off of the group."

Burden Sr. was chosen to take the lead because he was most capable, Faison said.

"We knew that he was the one that could really mastermind that type of thing and he has masterminded it all the way through," he said. "He saw things that we did not see and he led things that we had no idea how to lead, but he did."

His friend was also a man of his word, Faison said.

"He saw things that you could only imagine to see," he said. "He saw those things and he stepped out to get them. He worked hard, and he would accomplish things."

Terry Johnson, general manager of WHFL, worked with Burden Sr. for more than 30 years, watching the weekly telecast grow from a half-hour broadcast to an hour program. In the past two years, it went back to a half-hour as Burden's health declined. He estimated that more than 1,600 programs were produced locally through the Christian station, dating back to when it had been Gospel Television Goldsboro, on cable Channel 13.

"One of the greatest things I remember him saying was, 'Tell me something good about Jesus,'" he said.

He called Burden "a prince of a fellow" and said he had spent some time visiting Burden at home earlier this week.

"I came back to the office and told the staff his passing was going to be brief, it's not going to be long," he said.

They enjoyed a good working relationship, Johnson said, calling Burden a great community leader.

"His work and support of so many efforts in mission work -- churches and pastors and evangelists, he was able to bring people together," he said. "That's one of the things about Glenwood I will always remember. For me, to know Glenwood was to know Christ.

(Published in Goldsboro (NC) News-Argus on April 10, 2009, 1:46 PM (Reprinted with Permission)

God's Example in a Man

I will never forget the words of a man
Who imparted God's seed into my life's plan
Who spoke of wisdom from his heart
To encourage souls and inspire a spark
He made us think of how we could be better
With a spoken word, his memory travels
I remember the day he said to me
You think God started a work in you
He's not going to finish
Inspiring in me a breath of poetry
We must run this race that's set before us
A journey's end with family and friends
He set the standard for all humanity
Living life grand with honor and dignity
The greatest achievement a man can give
Is to live his life so others can feel
The heartbeat of God deep inside
Shared with others that love may abide
His life was an example, a spiritual accolade
Keeping the faith, with works he displayed
We will see him again
But not before our work is done
To hear Elder Burden say it
This race, you better run
We'll keep his spirit alive, now and forever

To God be the glory, who called our Elder
Glenwood Burden
Rest in Peace

"In Loving Memory of Elder Glenwood Burden"

In the Midst of Death

As I look at the obituaries, I see legacies of life
Children's children, children, offspring of life before life
A bloodline of forefathers and mothers
That has come before
Manifesting life, branded by a name
A characteristic, a voice
That speaks to generations to come of kindred spirits
Who paved the way for generations today
In the midst of death is an honorable spirit
That speaks in valor
The greatest accomplishment to achieve is death
Living life in accordance to eternal life
Death is honorable, to be revered, a suit unto our Father
The Ultimate home going
I entered the funeral home to view a body
I heard what many spoke of death
A chant of old by friends and relatives
I can't believe he's gone, I couldn't believe it when I heard
Be ye also ready...
Momma's holding up
Grandma always told her, she wanted her to be strong
Was but a few words of a descendant's song
Who broke in grief that was hard to bear
As her child cast blame, if only I were there
Did you know her, she passed away

Was the first words to leave her face
As I entered the building, my life changed forever
A friend of mine escaped her pain
Journeyed with our Father in heaven's domain
Words imparted aggravated my flesh
Weakened my body with a heavy chest
As I journeyed home, I laid it all on the altar
I cast my cares on the Author
And Finisher of our faith
I'll see them again someday at the pearly gates
Some I know for the fruits they bear
When I get to heaven they'll surely be there
The question that ponders at the door of my soul
To everyone in the funeral home
Is heaven
Your eternal home

Taming the Flesh

It angered me something fierce; to lose words imparted so
dear
This is the second time I've written this poem
The first one was lost, I nearly grew horns
Until a great revelation, as I starred at a blank page
Taming the flesh, calmed my rage
Above my spirit, cousin to my tongue, most unruly flesh
My life, you will not run
Will you deny my body shade where my soul stands
An internal warfare of my spirit and carnal man
If I stayed in the place where my spirit lay
Governing my body accordingly, there would be
No adversity
To write unto this testimony
Allocated safely were I and the spirit
My spirit gained, my body's domain
A mere mutter was my flesh
Until life called, I encouraged my body day and night
My body was my sight
To be more than whom I am, called the challenge in me
My flesh did rise and I could see, the enemy
In me
Oh, how I offend me
The mote in my eye, must I pluck it out
I searched myself as I journeyed in my soul

To find humility, a better part of me
While my flesh is greedy and my spirit's hungry
I must find a balance so neither is lonely
Until this is done, I will seek the Holy one
For in His name
My flesh will be tamed

Fasting in the Unknown

I fasted in the unknown and the Lord showed me of my blessing. Certainly, my flesh is weak and my spirit is willing. My mind is free from clutter and my spirit spoke to me as clear as I am. I had cast my cares on Him and wasn't to take them back. I thought of how I could encourage my situation to support what I needed in life. But I'm not to touch with my flesh what will spiritually manifest. I am to leave what I have given to the Lord with the Lord, a work He will finish, and I must wait. Previously prayed patience spoke to my spirit a word, taming the flesh is a quality that takes a lifetime to possess. Unwrap your mind from around your future. We have no hold on it, just limitations, for we can't perceive God's plan for us. We must get out of the way and stop playing it safe, wearing a banner of Pentecost if you will. Having a repetitive rendition of Christianity (routinely so). There're troublesome waters we have to travel to see our true potential and ourselves in God. It will feel uncomfortable to work in the physical body, trying to maintain spiritual strength. A greater level of meditation is needed to guide us righteously. Standing in the mist of our imperfections is a vulnerable place to be, sometimes causing us to want to run to our spiritual comfort zone, where everything feels good. Trusting God is key to conquering uncomfortable situations in our lives. To tame the flesh, we must realize our flesh, maintaining it by holding the Word of God in our heart, exemplifying it in our lives. Some things come but by prayer and fasting. These things I speak came by prayer and fasting. To listen with the spirit is to die to your flesh and physically be strengthened spiritually by God Himself who will feed you until you're full. Eat and drink life, strengthen your spiritual man, grow your physical man. Fasting in the unknown encourages unseen faith (faith before faith), if you will. I understand more than I knew in this life before. I may ask my Father of things to come through fasting and prayer, grace. I pray that my family is blessed beyond compare, with long life and longevity, a spiritual counteract intercepting impartations of wicked spirits that may come with works of iniquity to disrupt life. I pray that God bless life not yet conceived or heard of that He may encamp His angels and cover me and mine by His righteous blood that paid it all, binding iniquity and all its contingencies. A most powerful prayer to an Almighty God! I must pay attention so that I can see, so that I can hear, so that I can get what God has for me.

Evaluating My Reservation

I know where my treasures come from
But where are my treasures
I understand now
Someone once told me, when their work on earth is done
They'll be ready to go home
I thought that was contemptible
To want to leave this life in the midst of life
God has impressed upon my heart this day
A humble validity to such words that I must speak
To chase eternal life with a passion
Is like a jewel in a treasure box opened by its master
Admired as its own
With sparkles exemplifying faithfulness, will, and desire
For what's righteous and good
It is admirable to live life to its fullest
That suggests eternal life fulfilled
Know your journey that it extends from this life to the next
And harbor not on the affairs of this world
Achieve knowledge not impeding your spirit
That elevates you pass the things of this world
And its trivial pursuits
For we are governed by a higher power
To be revered and reverenced by our conscious behavior
Of faithfulness unto His righteousness
Affirming all is well with thee
Here and now, until forever

The day when we see our appraiser
And are polished in perfection, sustained from
Defectiveness
Healed from earthly wear
And cleaned with the countenance of His Divine
In the place where my treasure lie

"Spirit in the Water"

"Spirit in the Water"

My journey began May 25, 2009, Memorial Day. I was encouraged to visit a park several miles west of Goldsboro, North Carolina, which is said to be most inviting. A dear friend and I decided that we would journey -west and spend the evening at the park. When we arrived, it was as beautiful as all that is good. I began my journey as I crossed a nearby bridge admiring the grace of God and what beauty it held.

There was a light breeze and the sun was shining just right. I wouldn't have wanted to be anywhere else on this day. There was so much beauty there; I took pictures my entire journey. Mostly, I captured the beauty of nature; things that made my heart feel. I was blessed to have an opportunity to experience life fulfilled (To <u>live</u> life is to truly be fulfilled). I journeyed across the bridge, but not before I would stop at a nearby bench, where I would sit down and admire my surroundings. All that I felt was immense and overwhelming. My spirit and soul drank of the nectar that is life. The anointing in me was at home here. I felt a common ground with nature and my spirit. Some places I go and have never been before; I have to learn. I've been blessed to understand everything I need at these times is inside of me. God made us right! We are awesome by design.

I sat down for a few minutes and was on my way to see more of the beauty of nature. I walked further and finally exited the bridge where I would behold the most amazing trees I'd ever seen. They were phenomenal. I could almost feel the ancient spirits of time when I was near them as if spoken to my spirit. I felt as though I was among kings and queens of the earth. These trees have demeanors with strong presence that calls to our true history unscathed. There were so many of them to be admired and I was there to do just that.

As I passed this tree, I admired how profound the angle and the roots above the ground were. This was one of many trees that my eyes beheld of the beauty that is God. I feel mountains of stories told in the earth's surface. Songs of long ago that speak to our heritage, of ways and traditions

A Poet's Decree

of our people, man and woman alike; deeper still, immense revelations of kindred spirits that sing to my soul an anointed camaraderie of bloodlines extending from the beginning of time unto the present. We are cousin to the earth, a product of such with characteristics likewise, needing water to survive with the blessings of the sun as we weather the tests of times.

Along my journey I discovered that the ducks oftentimes retreated to dry land, where they attended to their business. Literally! As my friend and I walked a trail that extended the park, we found that we had to maneuver our steps to prevent stepping in poop. At this point I became a little discouraged. I wouldn't have mind if we were to turn around and traveled back a ways. I was encouraged to do otherwise, being that I've been challenging myself to step outside the box; I was enlightened to press on.

My friend and I walked a little further, where we were greeted with a warning and admired by the cutest little dog. We were told to be careful; there was a snake around the bend on the left side. Well, as soon as I heard snake, I took an about face as if to turn back. Again, my friend encouraged me otherwise, saying we could just walk around it. I wasn't so appeased this time, but I later came around, reiterating my previous suggestion, that I should step outside the box.

A Poet's Decree

We continued and were warned once again by two young men and a lady who had just passed the snake. As we approached the area where the snake lay, we could see it from a short distance. I immediately yelled back to one of the passing guys who came back to take a picture of the snake for me. I may as well not stop now! I had been taking pictures the whole journey. He obliged me and took the picture.

Before we would continue on, just horizontal from where the snake lay, there was the most beautiful sunset I've ever seen over the lake. I had to take a picture of it! We paused for a short while so that I could snap the shot. When I was done, I handed the phone to my friend to show her how beautiful it was; as I was handing it to her, before she could take the phone out of my hands, I looked at the picture. I saw something that moved everything inside of me and brought tears welling up inside. I placed my hands over my heart, then together as if to pray. There was what appeared to be the spirit of the Lord in the water.

On Memorial Day, May 25, 2009, we celebrated those who gave their lives for our country. I've been fortunate to realize a man who gave His life not only for this country, but the whole world. On this day, I received the greatest gift of all, what appeared as a manifestation of His Spirit.

Greater love hath no man…

A Poet's Decree

"Spirit in the Water"

Special Thanks

"Spirit in the Water" is dedicated to Ms. Erica Kennon without whom the story would not be told. Her perseverance and tenacity for the day was the biggest part in seizing the moments shared. Surely God used her as an instrument of His Divine love to impress upon my heart and share a place that is near and dear to hers. So many times we could have turned back, but we stayed the course because of her persistence and my need to step outside the box. Although this is true; God had a bigger plan and experience that we both will cherish for a lifetime. May God continue to bless and keep you in His sufficient grace as you journey in Him.

Friends for a Lifetime

I've prayed many prayers
And made many wishes
Until I met you, I didn't know
What I was missing
You've brought great joy
Into my life
My heart is bigger because of you
To acquire such a friend
Is to earn one too
To look in the mirror and see
It's not all about me
Weighing and considering
With understanding and respect
A treasure so rare, we don't normally get
Like a pearl from the ocean
Esteemed so high
Is where I hold you, a blessing from the sky
When the cares of this world have been so cruel
You were always there in good cheer or despair
Planting a seed whatever the need
A jewel I'll treasure with the finest care
With an appraisal that's imprinted upon my heart
Friends for a lifetime and eternity
You'll always be a special part of me

Introspection

Will You Still Preach Like That

You enter the sanctuary proclaiming
The salvation of the Lord
The saints stand to their feet in reverence to the choir
Marching in to "Anointing Fall Fresh on Me"
As their voices take a decrescendo
An officer of the choir speaks
Lord bless this choir and may we sing unto your joy
And may your anointing fall fresh today
The choir proceeds to take their seats
You may be seated, says the man of God
As I looked around the sanctuary at praying father's
Praying mothers
Brothers, sisters, and friends
There sits the first lady adorned with her children
And at the altar her man
Dressed in apparel befitting a king
A robe that drapes and high self-esteem
Preaching the word unto our deliverance
Is his heart's desire
Permeating the atmosphere with the Holy Ghost and fire
As tears rolled down my cheek
I looked to heaven so to speak
Thank You Lord is my cry, as humble as I stand
You are why
I live and breathe this day, in my heart I pray You'll stay

I lifted my head and wiped away my tears
The preacher preached and the saints cheered
Hallelujah! Was heard all over the place
Thank You Lord from every face
The man of God stood before the altar
Encouraging sinners not to falter
To come unto the Lord and He will give you rest
They kneeled at the altar, seven souls were saved
Seven joined the church
The man of God did the Lord's work
Preaching a Holy Ghost anointed sermon
That had the saints vertical, the service long
Then came the benediction and the saints would
Disburse home
Not before the church phone would ring
With a call for pastor
As we looked upon his face, he seemed to be displaced
His eyes filled with tears and his knees buckled
The phone dropped and the brothers hovered
Are you ok, grabbing the phone, is anyone there
The line was dead and pastor was in despair
After all that has been done and can't be taken back
When next Sunday comes, will he still preach like that

A Poet's Decree

Grace Away

There's a place not far away from happiness
Close to pain and repressed emotions
Lying dormant until an unknown time
That has become present
And prevalent with a vengeance
This would be grace away, which leads us to understand
His mercy
And a non-judgmental spirit
That invites forgiveness and looking in the mirror
While standing in another's shoes
In hopes to see ourselves
In affiliation with others
Who have fallen short of His glory
Aware of how we are where we are today
Because of circumstance
That can change in a moment's time
To drink of this word and be filled
Would conjure a belly of humility
Appropriate in life's time
That will set space in its place
Acknowledging we are kept
Only by God's grace

In Darkness

I woke this morning thankful to be here
In the midst of words said, help me Lord was my cry
To see pass my emotions with a spiritual eye
I rose from the place from whence I lay
Immersed in emotions that brought tears to my eyes
I must fight again a war waged in my youth
That would attack my mind and weaken my spirit
But, my flesh must move on
I adorned myself in Sunday attire
Prepped myself for someone higher
As I entered the church, I focused on why I was there
To deny myself, no burdens to bear
To my surprise, a guess speaker was there
To deliver the word to the shepherd's herd
I sat at times lost in space that God has given by His grace
In the spirit apart from my flesh
A mere revelation, I am happy at best
Until moments in time I saw my face, reality came
Into my space
I pondered a thought that spoke "in darkness"
Cousin to the topic the preacher would impart to us
Revival in the valley
A valley that descends fast and ascends slow
Descriptive of loneliness, depression, and darkness
A confirmation of affirmation
That I was on the same page and all was well

A word was sent to minister unto my soul
Ezekiel 37:1-10, prophesy to these bones and they shall live
Sometimes you have to speak a word over yourself
Speak to that darkness and tell it to be light

Spirits of the Mind

Hope reversed is a tragedy that pulls
You back into a box you had to come out of to dream
High waters of life that subsides in depth and tenacity
Empowered by innate inevitabilities
That invade emotional strength that dares you to dream
A mental tragedy that your mind conceived in hope
Not yet manifested, spiritually suggested
Hope reversed is a tragedy that pulls you back into a box
You had to come out of to dream
Devastating your spirit world
Introducing a rekindling of the spirit of failure
Inadequacy, self-worthiness, and purpose
Spirits of the mind come in all kinds
Jolting, provoking, sulking in tears
As you grasp for spiritual humanity, to keep your sanity
Hope reversed is a tragedy that pulls you back
Into a box you had to come out of to dream
Knowing, if you must succeed
You must come out again, and again, and again
To face the taunting of a possible win
That balloons into a stomach full of butterflies of the mind
Inspiring hope pass its manifestation
Encouraging dreams and races of endurance
Running pass renditions of inadequacies and failure
Until their spirit flees and hope is found again
And again, and again

A Poet's Decree

Never giving up on a possible taunting win
Hope reversed, a bittersweet end, that sends you back
To the beginning to see hope, only as you can
Conceiving dreams that inflate and burst
Unfortunately, until hope becomes reversed
A journey that transcends from the beginning of time
Into your lives and mine
Staying the course may have bumpy roads
And high streams
That pours into your cup an unsavory taste
You must not throw away, you must not waste
You must turn your bitter cup into a better taste
When hope becomes reversed and back again
Is your reason for your stand
Knowing
It gets hard sometimes fighting
Spirits of the mind

The Majority of the Time

I spend alone
Absent of physical contact and conversation
Not by sole choice of course, but a will within a will
That encourages a spiritual covering that protects me
From not only myself, but others who mean me no good
I'm overwhelmed at times by the separation and degree
With an innate understanding not to master the borders
That has spiritually been laid
So, after I squirm in almost fits of myself
I'm calm by my Knower and life, that lessens
My internal rage
I accept my place with or without the presence of another
Suggesting proper place and understanding
To everything there is a season
This season is for growth and spiritual prosperity
Alluding to abundant life destined from the start
Not before the ground work is done in my life
And I know who I spiritually am
Suggesting, spending time with my heavenly Father
And Maker who has called me unto this day
To stare prosperity in the face and see its consequences
To look at success and know its objective
To seek my inheritance and tame my heart
Knowing it's my Maker that has called me unto this day
The reason for my season of growth

And spiritual prosperity
A time to be prepared to receive what thus sayeth the Lord
Amen

Let Them Go

I left their presence, but didn't let them go
I think of them even though they're far from me
I have to let them go, so I can be
I think of them here and there for sure
I must let their spirits go imparted to me,
Keeping them righteously
Their smells, their answers, their suggestions
Born again, into a new phase of me
Above the spirit of my head is where I want to be
Safe from harm, my Father and me
A place where I'm suggested as just, just to achieve
In minds that conceive, the gifts God's planted
Deep inside of me
Encouraging me effortlessly, the epitome of places we are
And soon will be
We are creatures of the same cause
Cousins to success, sisters to the fall
Constantly standing through it all
I want to be in this place to encourage a transformation
Of my mind and spirit
I must leave this place that has been my guts and glory
I must leave this place that said I wouldn't make it
I must leave my past where I found it and be transformed
By the renewing of my mind
I must journey among the spiritual bodies in the plan

And soar among the clouds, conquering plutonic measures
Big and small
There's a place that's waiting for me
Cousin to success, sister to the fall
I must endure
I will obtain it all
Who will I share with, who will care, for I left them all
Behind, so-called friends, no one's there
I will call upon the few that has adorned my life
No matter what the journey
To share with me in this place I want to be
I will not stop until my journey's end
Some say less is more, when you're counting friends
Or you can count them all on one hand
Quit to the contrary in this journey among friends
That will soar with me to greatness
As I seek my Father's plan

New Year's Eve

My hands are in the air
Others perception of me will be as they just
My hands are in the air
I'm no longer considering the reconstruction of their minds
To exemplify and encourage them to see me differently
The obvious degradation of wavering impressions
Of spiritual impartations
Are fathomed when I'm in their presence
I no longer wish to prepare myself to be more in their eye
Nor do I inspire for such contingencies
I don't care anymore
My hands are in the air, I see now
What I'm supposed to see
This is why I fight no more, nor do I care what others see
The war has been waged and the fight is not mine
Whatsoever is bound on earth, shall be bound in heaven
Whatsoever is loosed on earth, shall be loosed in heaven
"Spirits of the mind come in all kings
Jolting, provoking, sulking in tears
As you grasp for spiritual humanity
To keep your sanity"
A cause of perpetuated ills manifested on lips
Evolutions of sounds and voices
That's found me on the mouths of strangers
My hands are in the air from this horrid affair

A Poet's Decree

There's a way this battle is won, there's a way
To stop the song
Chants of yesterday, but a new day has come
Chants of yesterday, silence everyone
My life is mine, my voice hovers over
My life is mine, dawn! New Year
Goodbye old chime

Shake It Off

Don't worry about how tired you've been
Don't worry about how many times
You've been in this place
Don't worry about what it seems like
Shake it off
Shift in another gear or it will consume you
Shift in another gear, no one's going to save you
Shift in another gear with tenacity and
Shake it off
Everything you need is inside of you
Shift in another gear, it'll come true
Try yourself some faith
Give yourself some love
Be gone with self-pity, be gone grudge
Be gone unfaithfulness consumed by love
Hell be gone, hell be gone
Misery, misery has no home
The day has come, you've been sought out
It's time to be quiet without a doubt
From questions, irritations, reasons, and wonders
Hope and fantasies, put asunder
In remission from pain, an overwhelming cause
That stricken solace
A medium that renders calm, into a tired peace
Shaken Off

A Poet's Decree

Beautiful Hearts

The enemy roams to and fro in the earth seeking whom he may devour and has devised a strategy using the idea of love so that we can't see how much he hates us. A relationship that is doomed from the start, entertained by two longing for love will endure pain, compromise, and ultimate denial for the sake of love and a sense of fulfillment. Compromise doesn't have to be bitter and selfless, but maybe an avenue to understand that someone isn't the one for you and vice versa. True happiness is not what we think makes us happy. True happiness is what makes us happy. Some happiness inspires for moments then subsides to naught (an illusion of happiness). True happiness is a constant that wins every time never failing. Perhaps, I adore the beauty of the sun shining through trees as the wind blows the leaves. It revives in me essentials ignited every time my senses are aware. True happiness is love felt without a touch, very powerful and weightless! Maybe even the immense freedom space gives when traveling to a different place or in the eyes of a child just beginning to walk; the joy of comforting someone who displays they've been touched reaching the very core of you, your heart. That's true happiness!

Society has stolen happiness, labeling it into what it should be. Happiness from the beginning of time has been and came without a dim. Money can't buy love or happiness. People have been fooled, new generation and old, looking for happiness in clout, which supposed to bring self-worth and stature. New age, old age, there's nothing new under the sun.

Love has been turned into many things, such as the love of money. Because of centuries of the earth being abused and manufactured products, pesticides and so forth compromises the agriculture. We're made of dust and its elements and are foreign from whence we came, because of the pollutants some have manufactured. The cares of this world will choke the word right out of you. We live in a Babylonian society that doesn't see you, but seeks to so-call legitimize you by its standards. We have to buy what is free. We have to buy who we are. We have to buy the elements from which we're made producing what we naturally need. High-end whole food stores take no pause in selling us right back to us (live food, organic etc.). To be able to avoid this is to afford this. While others live and think anything can be purchased. However, rather it's for the love of someone or something, to a beautiful heart, true happiness doesn't cost a thing.

Social Sobriety

Indirect, external oppressions of the world
Rides thick and runs deep into the carnal man
Who's built a fence around life so he can live
And the cares of this world he can't feel
Ignoring fashion, fade and trend
External factors that never end
But transcends to our children, who make amends
To have what's in
He'd rather thrive on love that makes him feel
Alive, good, and real, things in life that don't cost a thing
But, the world says you're nothing
If you don't have that bling
Fine cars, and a house, wearing nothing less than the best
A standard he can't yet meet, a place his destiny seeks
New eyes have found him a heart within
Yearning for more, needing to mend
So the cares of this world won't do him in
When the place his destiny seeks is fulfilled
His heart will be in place to deal
Enjoying the finer things in life
With or without, he can depend
On the fervent heart
Of a righteous man

The Day After

What must I do to have my words true
To have words travel
From the beginning of my emotions
To the end of how I feel
I am comprised of much more than myself
With contingencies that descend
Before my existence and ascend to the last seed
Of my kindred generation
Oh how I'm revealed, Oh how I must live
There's so much to gain and so much to give
A responsibility founded upon my heart's desire
To press pass selfish desires
Of assumed completions that will only profit me none
However, I've opened a door
That allowed me to see within sight
I am my people, responsible indeed
To share this vision
Live this life, even fight this fight
I am my people responsible indeed
For every seed
That weighs heavy on my soul
Speaking as such
That I should intercede on behalf of their lives
Cares and pressures of this world
That have overwhelmed some and taunted others

A Poet's Decree

Jesus is the way, the truth, and the light
It is His will we all have sight
To brighten the way that others might
I have seen some today
That I may shed some tomorrow
And pray for days to come
These are the seeds of Amaziah and Mable Lane
That has replenished the earth a part of the fullness thereof

My Egypt Experience

Absolute Silence & Signature
Absolute silence, panic was my first experience
A foreign place, immerged in me blame, pity, and question
Didn't I sow enough seeds to reap the desire that I am
Wasn't I a friend indeed, a shoulder if needed
Oh, how I wanted this cup from me
The staggering moments of silence that filled my days
I thought of ways I could satisfy this place
But the desire for my Father's will
Is bigger than my conclusions
After squirming in fits of myself
Many questions subsided upon renditions
Of absolute silence
For many days my thoughts were my conversation
Company I never thought I'd keep
An uncanny degree of separation
My signature is upon this place
Kept by God, I learn to embrace
Humility, patience, and selflessness
He showed me where I came from and all its contingencies
How my storms have been my shelter
Seeking Him through it all
Each day became something new, a new reason
A new way, a new opportunity
God's provisions supplied my every need

A Poet's Decree

In the most unorthodox ways
It was awkward, never knowing how He would provide
Use to figuring out how or where ends would meet
I was in a place where He met my needs
When He met my needs
Many ways did He bless me
Through people, places, and conversations
I praised Him despite of depression
I never gave up although the enemy attacked my mind
With negative thoughts
I learned perseverance and He is what I want most
Capitalizing on what I have and as Bob Marley once said
Emancipate your mind from mental slavery
Finding blessings in many places
My Egypt experience has been a wilderness
Where I spiritually communicated
And spent time with God
I feel civilization ahead, my deliverance is near
But this place brings such humility and recognition
Of valuable, priceless, incomparable things in life
I wouldn't have seen
If it had not been for my Egypt experience
I must find out when I am delivered, my life
Will I sustain in my heart the experiences of this season
A place of humility, where I'm closest to God

What Has Life Done to You

Is the heartbeat and present passion
Lingering in the presence of life
Looking out into vast places, far and between
Manifestations of life, past and present signatures
Staining the human anatomy, speaks to my spirit to write
Out of our mother's womb
We challenged the enemy with life
From our first words spoken to our first steps taken,
We've been a target
To be sifted like the herbs of the field
I turned my head like pages to a book, as was like
The past and present day
Searching for pages in between to fill the space
Delivering many afflictions calling us unto this day
To rally in discernment, empowering over he who
Roams the earth seeking whom he may devour
A visual is my first impression, conversation will
Teach the lesson
I pondered to fill the spaces in between
I must begin with myself, testifying of adversities
The enemy has dealt
Attacking my mind and present health
Giving me a word to help someone else
Is the greatest desire that I am
Without inclination and many moons, my journey began

A Poet's Decree

That would scar me twice in the same place
Take my womb and disfigure my face
Leaving me with a name I dare claim
In the same rendition space and time
A biopsy of my eye and left armpit was mine
That sung a song, an unpleasant chime
And was given a name I dare claim
Cancer, in carcinoma, achieved the biggest test
A bilateral mastectomy removed both breast
Still it wasn't over and can't be undone
I turned my head to see
What has life done
I passed him today, for a lifetime I have
Like the enemy who seeks, he walked to and fro
I guess the enemy followed everywhere he would go
To steal a page and leave spaces in between
If restored would redeem, a six foot three
Frame of a man with broad shoulders and arms swinging
He wore glasses that signified and had calve muscles
The same
A strong strapping man, until the enemy came
I laid my eyes upon him; it felt like someone had
Gutted my soul
Stole my breath, absence the brilliance of God
And left the frame of a man to stand
With a cane and frail body
Walking still, to and fro, with glasses that signify
And life speaks

What has life done to you
I turned my head, like pages to a book
As was like the past and present day…

A Brilliant Concept I Suppose

We were born in sin and shaped in iniquity, given a choice
Influenced, cultivated, and taught a way of life
Until a day of discernment, we would acknowledge God
As our Master, Creator, and Savior
Thus, a rebirth in the earth
Old things were passed away, all things have become new
The tone has been set to take back everything
The enemy has stolen
Through seasons of identity theft
A brilliant concept I suppose
Out of our mothers' wombs, we were met
With any conceivable spirit imaginable
The possibility of committing any sin
Jesus bared on the cross
A liar, a cheat, a thief, an adulterer are but a few
Only by God's grace, we are saved from the
Torturous snares of the enemy
Who says to our youth
I'll show them all they can see
I'll give them less than can be
Emulating, imitating, and conjugating
Enslaving gifts of freedom
When I'm old enough I can walk like you
Talk like you, even curse too
No one can stop me 'cause I'm grown now

Twisting my hips, painting my lips, hanging out late
This is the life, I'm grown now says me
Something to look forward to, seeing all that you do
Everything around me says what I am supposed to be
My momma did it, my cousin did it, my aunt did it too
Before I'm old enough, I'll start smoking too
I'm wondering if I'm going to finish school
Because becoming a lady
Means having a baby
And moving out soon
Or maybe even staying home with mom
My sister and my cousin did it, can't be no harm
Maybe I'll get a boyfriend and a place in the projects
We won't starve; I hear the welfare gives out checks
I'll have it made; I'll be on my own doing good
That sounds nice, even if for the rest of my life
A brilliant concept I suppose
An illusional, delusional perpetual cycle
From the beginning of time
Created to smell good and leave you blind
Blind to the ways of the enemy's chime
A familiar normality conceived as the way, the only way
To grow up and become something of consequence
Amongst your peers
Orchestrated strategically, confining and stealing years
Saturated burdens and eyes full of tears
Reflections of life
And years never lived

A Poet's Decree

The Root

Outraged at what money has done to my people
In and out of convenient stores
For loose cigarettes and beer
Cheap wine and cholesterol filled chicken
A momentary fix to a hunger pain of malnourishment
Waiting to get the ultimate fix
A hit
That's what they call it
Hard hitting blow after blow
Taking down whole families, destroying friendship
Crack cocaine, white snow
Infesting my people so no one will grow
Thus, the scenario of dealers, hustlers
Drug boys, drug lords
Illusions in the ghetto, they got it going on
Cars, money, silver and gold
Illusions of grandeur, God help their souls
Impressing upon children unfortunate with desire
To have what they see
While drowning, drowning
In poverty

Holy Spirit

Stop sucking what cannot blow in heart
Drink from life and be full
Let them have what they can drink of thee
And when you're spiritually tired
And physically weak
Find solace in thee
Many have come to suck the life out me
A hunger that thirst beyond sin and iniquity
That cannot be filled nor can it mend
The wayward heart of the sinner man
Three times a day he fed his flesh
And his spirit man is dormant at rest
Drink from life and be full
In the sacred temple your soul resides
In the presence of God, your Father's eyes
Anointing! Anointing! My spirit arises
Filled once again that they may drink of me
The spirit of my Father, many men thirst for thee
Many men search for thee
Just feel a part of thee
Even if it's inside of me

A Poet's Decree

Uninvited

Unaware of how I'd gotten to this place
Certainly, cunning and well orchestrated I suppose
I found myself afflicted with despair
That plagued my spirit and weighed heavy on my flesh
Sickened from oppression
And the cares of this world intensified
In time, I became numb to God's discipline imparted to me
Feeling foreign and a bit overwhelmed
I commanded myself, struggling to seek deliverance
Still it wasn't over
By my own admission and contingencies
I found my thoughts afflicted
Discomforting my flesh
Familiar spirits of the past had resurfaced as though
I had committed a sinful act
Revealing to me
Even as a man thinks
He can choose what will be

His Omnipotence

Gazing into the heavens, immense depth and power
Overwhelmed my poise
Free of myself, tone deaf to noise, my spirit spoke
In one accord
Great is our God who created the heavens and the earth
Great is our God, to everything gave birth
Even greater still to behold the earth
Surrounded by His grace, empowered by His omnipotence
Our God is here in the midst of the trees, near every leaf
That catches the breeze
Before a storm cloud and setting sun
His magnificence unveil
His beauty is won
In awe of His creations, brilliant perfection
A work in the heavens, found beauty in the earth
Our lives, an example, His creation from dust
New life He breathes, on the heavens and the earth
Great is our God
To everything gave birth
The Greatest Creator ever, died for you and me
That we might have life, more abundantly
Above all we can fathom, more than we can see
Our deepest desires, our hearts sincerity
Fulfilled in us, God's prophesy
And the heavens did speak mountains in the earth

A Poet's Decree

Dominion to mankind our Father's worth
Mighty is the Lamb, Ruler of the heavens and the earth
Mighty is the Lamb, to everything gave birth

Witness Then

There're so many people talking about what God wants
In their own might
A positive testimony is lost amongst intellectual jargon
We all want to be the principal child of God
Then I suggest, immense humility, absolute silence,
And death
To obtain the peace in wisdom that God gives her
As should be given to others
What God has to say is very clear, brilliant, and unwitty
No cause for refrain
The enemy is the author of confusion
And an ego should be far from a witness
Many are hungry for the Word of God
And will stand there
Listening to hints of what God has given
In efforts to feed their soul
Meanwhile, a spiritual endeavor
Has become a carnal pleasure

Prophetic Poetry

They Say You Can
Write Your Own Ticket

I think I'll write mine
I'm going to write my way out unto many blessings
I'm empowered by the Spirit of God and the words I speak
The many adversities I've encountered
I'm sharing them with whoever will listen
Weakening the chains of the enemy, calling him out
Speaking of adversities and how God brought me out
Rerouting negative intentions of the enemy past myself
With a sincere heart to help someone else
When the words are out and it is done
God will bless them one by one
And unto the world this seed
He will spread to many hearts
That seek to be fed
No one can stop this
Not even I
Who wrote the book
From an anointed eye
These words will give unto my bosom
The rhythm of this world
More earthly treasures than I can bear
In this time of great prosperity
My journey has brought me to this page
Molded me unto this day

So I rejoice in the fruits of this life
To a day that has been achieved unto my life
Many seeds that's been sown to return home
I'm rich, body and soul
Amen

The Whole Armor of God

(Close to Unique Teere Tomorrow)

I have decided to completely surrender to God
There's a place that needs to die
I wrote "Let them Go" that physically encouraged me
I had left their presence
But I had to let their spirits go imparted to me
Those behaviors that compliment and acknowledge
Recognition and agreement
I must die
Therefore, I have asked my Lord and Savior
Jesus Christ
To come into my life and clean me up
I do not wish for my past to find agreement with me
I desire that God is my first and last subject
The premise of my life is that my spirit
Has free reign and my flesh
Knows its domain
The beginning of a great transformation
In my life

Prophesy of Restoration

God is restoring my mind to brilliance
To be all I was put here to be
Because I've been faithful
Through the test of times, I am redeemed
I shall speak fluently the work of God
Because I've acknowledge what the enemy
Has set out to do, binding it, and shared with others
The shackles and contingencies have been disengaged
Causing behaviors acquired for many years
To be released and freed from me
I'm entering into a different dispensation
A rebirth, with new eyes, and new mind
To press forward and do the will of the Lord
Eyes have not seen, ears have not heard
Nor has it entered the hearts of man
The good things in store for those that love Him
My destiny is here
(Close to a unique teere tomorrow)

A Poet's Decree

"No Mountains to Climb" suggests removing obstacles out of the way before they occur, empowering self-worthiness, esteem, and compatibility. Some were fortunate to have those in their lives to disengage certain contingencies by imparting knowledge and experiences that constitutes positivism needed to aspire for the best.

Although this is true; those who have not found such a position, God, the source and Creator of your being has your position that will set you in place to be available for yourself and your spiritual destiny (Your Unique Teere tomorrow) when God positions you in a higher spirit realm. To take back what the enemy has stolen; we must go back to when he took it, know what he took, place and time, and acknowledge what has been done with a conscious mind. "Out of our mother's womb, the enemy has been trying to kill us. We were born in sin and shaped in iniquity." Although this is true, the Lord was there as well and still is.

The enemy went to work on us in our youthfulness, when we had not even fully developed, when our minds were impressionable and we were trying to understand who we are and what life is about. Because of the early entry of the enemy; he has fooled many into thinking that bad habits that have plagued us for a lifetime are who we are. Not so! There are those who possess the spirit of inadequacy, alcoholism, doubt, fear, etc. that originated during a time when you weren't equipped to handle life's daggers. There may have been a certain environment you were put in that caused certain behaviors that imparted into your spirit. You have to examine yourself, your life and God will reveal to you a journey to release. This is why a personal relationship with God is detrimental to completion. Once God has opened certain doors in your life, providing understanding; you will be set in a place where you are available for your spiritual destiny, a rebirth into a different dispensation.

Hearing the Voice of God

"Listening to the Spirit"

The enemy has imitated the voice of God
That it may appear evil from the beginning of time
I heard a voice in my dream that sounded like
What we portray as the enemy
But spoke brilliant intercession
"Separate times you feel vs. emotions you own"
My spirit tried and saw that it was good
The Bible says the Lord has a voice of many waters,
Which is very deep
As was the voice in my dream
The way I feel is what I know and have accepted
In my Knower
My emotions are the ways I've felt
Throughout my whole life
When something takes place that triggers
The voice was an example (deep) to separate what I feel
From the emotions I own
We're taught that voice is the voice of the enemy
Therefore, imparting resistance
That spoke the wisdom of God
My feeling is deep in my Knower
The wisdom of God is bestowed upon me
While emotions heard a deep voice

Portrayed as the enemy
Triggering emotions I own because of the
Rhythm of the world and time
However, my spirit discerned a righteous spirit
That spoke growth and prosperity
Into my being

It's My Run

The closer I get to God
The higher I'm going to stand
My spiritual constitution
There were those who have tried to sow into the seeds
God has planted inside of me
Life's agenda has taken them in a different direction
It's time for my Father and me
It has ended and it has begun
Now, to God be *all* the glory

The Warriors Are in the Wilderness

Jesus went into the synagogue
Walked in the wilderness for the most part
Proclaimed saints of God are going
To the synagogue, routinely so
Unfortunately, there're too many people in the church
The spirit of the Lord is quenched in their presence
He can barely enter His house
Thus, many saints are reverting to the wilderness
Where they can hear the voice of God
And be led by His omnipotence
For they can't be reached inside the church
Because the people refuse to die, that His spirit may arise
God's will, will be done
Even if He has to send the saints into the wilderness
To teach them His prophetic way
A brilliant rendition of there's nothing new under the sun
A great manifestation is in the land
Many are called, but few are chosen and unto the chosen
Are the saints who have hidden the Word of God
In their hearts
That it may sustain them in their walk
As they encounter spiritual counterparts of the body
That imparts keys and nuggets of wisdom
Confirming God's will

Strengthening and empowering the warriors
In the wilderness
Who possess the anointing of old
That makes way for God's Word to manifest
And His works done
In my name shall you cast out demons
In my name shall you heal the sick
In my name shall you raise the dead
In my name
Therefore; one must die
Amen

New Year's Day 2011, 11:38 A.M.

My spirit spoke to me in silence
Conscious and unconscious reaping
For the past year I have consciously reaped my very being
God has allowed me to see my life in retrospect
That gives a certain demeanor of control
And attentiveness to my person
A rhythm to bear
For the past few weeks I've not understood
The transformation
In my journey that unconsciously conjures
Emotions and events I thought were far from me
That I surely do not wish to entertain
Many things were called out
During my year of ultimate reaping
Which I thought were in their proper places
But there is a shaking going on
And I have no control over it
I am unconsciously reaping myself
And emotions that triggered throughout my life
Therefore, it seems I have no control
Because it's happening at will
But my spirit is keeping me steady
To endure this journey
On the other side of this reaping
Is uncontrolled blessings

Operating at will as well
To God be the glory
Who created the heavens and the earth

"As Was in My Dream"

The devil is on the prowl
Seeking whom he may devour
The prince of the air has plotted his plan
On every soul and infested the land
Even every sin he imparts, to leave your focus dark
Unto the trash you dispense, will seep into the land
The hell of the sins of the day, on every soul to prey
Panic is in the land, people scatter to get away
Even myself to higher ground, there's chaos all around
No sin befell me, as I wondered though town
Looking for a way out through the courtesy of a man
Who said he would do everything he can
He yelled for his car and sanctioned for his keys
Entered a doorway from a man he would retrieve
When he returned to me, only evil I see
One man yelled, the kid wasn't crazy who said
The devil is in this town, I got to leave
The spirit is thick, manifesting in trees
Targeting the poor and unfaithful, to his success
Setting up shop in the heart of hell, a designated spot
To tear them apart
No one would be the wiser, setting up shop
In cess pool of heartache, bitterness, and pain
Painting a picture of how it all will be better again
An anchor to hold on to, while he plotted

To manipulate you
Carefully altering their minds, impressing sin of the times
When the web he wove spins
They never knew what came in
Transformed for hell, while others scramble to bail
When this secret is revealed
He chases heel to heel
As they run to get away
There're runners every way

Blink

Your mind will take you wherever you want to go
There was a man who sold alcoholic beverages
That had no alcohol in it
The idea suggested behavior that alcohol would impart
But it was all in their minds
People will sell anything, even a stuffed animal
Full of maggots as long as it feels soft to the child
And some will allow their child to play with it
Lift your hands in surrounding areas
Of God's plan for your life
There may be some who seek to abuse you
And your purpose
Because of the gifts you possess
Praise Him through your circumstance and you will
Become the best at what you do for
The glory of His kingdom
There's none other that get up in the morning
For what you get up for
We are designated
For what God wants us to do
Grow omniously in Christ

Kindred Spirit

I'll tell you what I know, only what I know
Our trials are to make us stronger, and ultimately grow
Greatness is a gift that's expressed in our journey
Many adverse times, winding roads and some that bind
For moments in time
To teach life's lesson, then unwind
Into narrow roads as we make way
For our Father
To mold us unto the day
Signatures our bodies, the human anatomy
Mentally receiving, spiritually believing
Signs in the body read
Of journeys of faith, and perseverance
Strength no man gave and can take away
How we chose life than to wither away
As the enemy nagged at our apparent affliction
But to no avail
We refused to be victims
We chose to stand through the storms
Providing tough winds and bodily harm
That faith would heal
And victory won
Chin up
Don't despair, we're cousins of affliction
Remnants of the past, cause trouble never last

I'll tell you what I know, only what I know
We weathered the storms, withstood the tests of times
Journeyed winding roads and some that binds
Discovered unknown strength in the quietest parts
Of our minds
Places God revealed unknown to mankind
He gave us revelations no man can take away
Embedded into our spirits, molded us unto the day
With a powerful testimony ordained by God
That will pierce the soul of many with the anointing
That lies within
And the wisdom He dispenses
I'll tell you what I know, only what I know
We were chosen for the challenge, because we could win
An example had to show us
Before the victory's in
We are so much and have so much to be discovered
Is why I'll tell you what I know
What has been revealed
When it reaches your heart
May you begin to heal

A Poet's Decree

Destiny

May we soar from the floor, from the grace
Of gravity, to space
Seeking and reaching, pulling and yielding to face
An explosion of oneself of purpose and greater wealth
Bestowed in life, before the belly of the womb
Parallel intersections that cross and pass
As you reach for relevance from the first and the last
Impressing impressions upon your life
That jolts in place in an instant
Causing revelations of relevance
That spews into a conjugation of purpose and significance
As you are awaken, life has new meaning
Now that you've found yours
In a place where body meets space and time
That holds still for no one
For parallel intersecting roads speaks volumes to some
And others never get told
Of their life's journey
That was to plug in place
For they chose the cares of this world
Instead of running my Father's race

Contact Information

The author is available for poetry readings and book signings. You may contact her at (919) 396-3688.

You may also send her an email to:
breathofapoet@yahoo.com

For information on ordering copies of *A Poet's Decree*, please contact the author at the address above, or you may contact:

Kingdom Living Publishing
P.O. Box 660
Accokeek, MD 20607
publish@kingdomlivingbooks.com
301-292-9010

Also by Pamela M. Young

(ISBN: 978-0-9799798-2-8)

Available at www.amazon.com, www.barnesandnoble.com, or
wherever books are sold.

CPSIA information can be obtained
at www.ICGtesting.com
Printed in the USA
FFOW03n2241161216
30416FF

9 780996 808910